PIRATE

How To Use This Book

Fill the two pirate scenes - *On The Deck* and *The Captain's Cabin* - with the stickers from coloured sticker pages. It's up to you where you put them!

•

Read the captions on the *A Pirate's Life* and *Into Battle* pages and, using the labels next to the stickers, choose the images from the white sticker pages that you think best fit the available spaces.

•

Your stickers can be stuck down and peeled off again. If you are careful, you can use your Pirate stickers more than once.

•

You can also use the stickers to decorate your own books, or for project work at school.

DK

London, New York, Melbourne,
Munich, and Delhi

Written and edited by Kate Turner
Designed by Jon Hall
Illustrated by Roger Harris

First published in Great Britain in 2004 by Dorling Kindersley Limited,
80 Strand, London, WC2R 0RL
A Penguin Company

DK Australia
250 Camberwell Road, Camberwell, Victoria 3124

04 05 06 07 08 10 9 8 7 6 5 4 3 2 1

Copyright © 2004 Dorling Kindersley Limited

All rights reserved. No part of this publication may be reproduced, stored in a retrieval system, or transmitted in any form or by any means, electronic, mechanical, photocopying, recording, or otherwise, without prior written permission of the copyright owner.

ISBN 1-4053-0320-4

Colour reproduction by Media Development and Printing Ltd, UK
Printed and bound by L. Rex, China

Dorling Kindersley would like to thank:
British Museum, Board of Trustees of the Armouries, Hull Museum, Mary Evans Picture Library, Musee de Saint-Malo, Museum of London, National Maritime Museum, Rye Town Council Guy Ryecart, The Trustees of the V&A, Viking Ship Museum Oslo, Wilberforce House.

All other images © Dorling Kindersley.
For further information see www.dkimages.com

Discover more at
www.dk.com

A Pirate's Life

Daily life for pirates was gruelling, hazardous, and boring. On board, the men would often fall sick, fights were common, and misdemeanours were brutally punished by the ship's officers. Of course, all pirates faced death if they were ever brought to justice.

In for a flogging
The captain of a pirate ship commanded the respect of his crew, and might punish disobedience with a flogging.

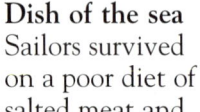

Dish of the sea
Sailors survived on a poor diet of salted meat and hard bread. But the Caribbean once abounded with tasty turtles, which were a good source of fresh meat.

Fresh produce
Hens provided fresh meat, and the eggs they laid were a good source of protein. The hens could be kept alive in the hold until required.

Real-life pirate
Captain Howell Davis was a daring 18th-century pirate. Born in Wales and raised on a ship, he used his pleasant manner to fool many people into giving up their cargo. He plundered many treasure ships.

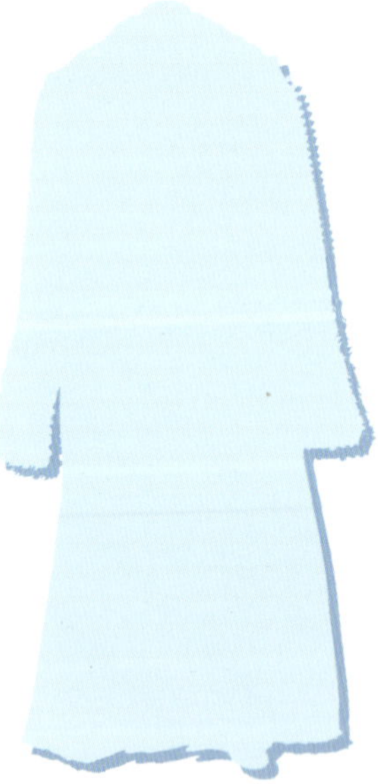

Licensed to steal
Some governments issued special letters, granting ships' crews license to plunder enemy merchant ships. These crews were known as privateers.

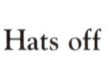

Bottles of grog
Before leaving port, pirates would stock up on beer and wine. As well as being a welcome tipple, alcohol survived in storage for far longer than water, which soon turned stale and too rank to drink.

Hats off
Real pirates were usually dressed in rags, and only changed their clothes when they had stolen new ones. This three-cornered 'tricorn' hat might have been worn by a pirate captain.

Luxury get-up
Not all pirates were from poor backgrounds. Sir Francis Verney, an English gentleman, became a pirate in the early 17th century and used to wear this plush cloak. He was captured and put into slavery by a rival gang of pirates.

Turtle

Grappling iron for pulling in an enemy ship

Ring with skull-and-crossbones

Limes

Chicken

17th-century cutlass

Crowsfeet or caltrop

Rat on a rope

Spanish gold doubloons

Flintlock pistol

Musket balls

Leather purse and coins

Bartholomew Roberts' flag

17th-century liquor bottle

Anchor

Wealthy pirate's cloak

Flogging

Anne Bonny, female pirate

Gems

Gold seal ring

Emerald pendant

Captain Jack Rackham's crossed swords flag

Pirate Henry Avery's Jolly Roger

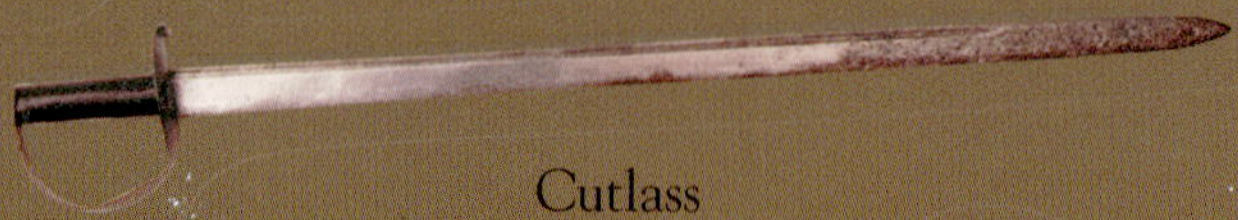

Cutlass

Map of Madagascar

Sack of flour

Sailing rope

Parrot

Spanish gold doubloons

Water barrel

Treasure chest

Fictional pirate Long John Silver

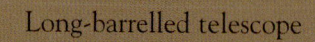

Long-barrelled telescope

Stolen gold coins

Heavy cannon with bronze barrel

Backstaff used to calculate latitude

Blackbeard's flag

Cannon balls

Dividers for chart measurements

Rat

Privateer's ship – a converted fishing vessel

Lantern

Gems

Sailors' biscuits – 'hard tack'

Axe

17th-century French treasure chest

19th-century rapier

Dashing pirate captain

Letter from the King

Handcuffs

Gold rings

Rose-sapphire cross

"The Swallow"

Viking head carving

Compass bowl

Tricorn hat

Powder horn

Dagger

Iron gibbet cage

A public hanging

Marooned sailor

19th-century glove puppet

Neck collar and chain

Bold Welsh pirate Howell Davis

Ready, action!
Pirates made popular characters for screen and stage – and also for puppet theatres. This 19th-century wooden-headed puppet, wearing sailor's attire and carrying a cutlass, portrays a typical English pirate.

Desert island risks
Sometimes shipwrecked sailors became marooned on islands. One privateer, Alexander Selkirk, spent five years alone on a South Pacific island. Surprisingly, he liked it there and didn't want to leave! Selkirk was the model for the storybook legend, Robinson Crusoe.

Uninvited guests
Rats were an ever-present problem on all ships. They spread disease, ate the food supplies at an alarming rate, and gnawed through just about anything, even the timbers of the ship itself!

A severe warning
After a pirate was caught and hanged, his body would be put inside an iron cage, called a gibbet. This prevented his relatives from retrieving the body for burial, and served as a warning to others who were thinking of taking up piracy.

Clapped in irons
Handcuffs and shackles were used on captured pirates or slaves to prevent escape. Some slaves were chained together in a 'chain gang' while they worked, and kept in ankle fetters at night. Runaway slaves sometimes joined pirate ships for a better life.

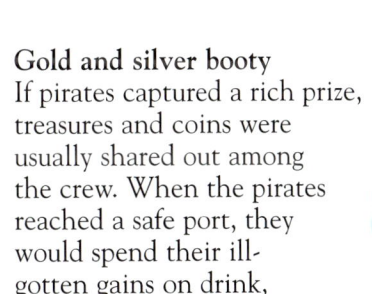

Gold and silver booty
If pirates captured a rich prize, treasures and coins were usually shared out among the crew. When the pirates reached a safe port, they would spend their ill-gotten gains on drink, gambling and women.

Traditional execution
Pirates who were caught were given a public hanging on wooden gallows. Great crowds would gather, eager to get a good view. The hanging rope was made of hemp, which is where we get the grim saying 'dancing the hempen jig'.

Natural medicines
In 1753 it was discovered that people who ate certain fresh fruits didn't get scurvy, a crippling disease. After this, ships always carried fruit in the hold, especially limes and lemons, which both contain vitamin C.

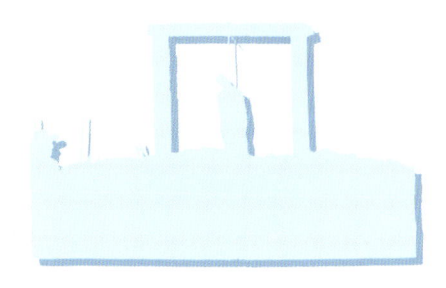

Into Battle

Piracy has existed in nearly every historical era. Some pirates were deserters from the navy; others were privateers, whose misdeeds were actually sponsored by their nation's government. Battles were fierce, for the potential loot could turn poor sailors into millionaires.

The mother of all ships
This huge ship, *The Swallow*, was used by the British Navy to overpower pirate vessels. Most pirates preferred a fast, light, sleek ship for a quick attack and getaway.

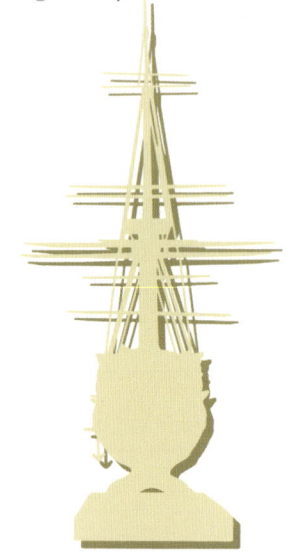

Cruel cutthroats
The cutlass was first used by buccaneers to hunt cattle, whose meat they supplied to ships. The short, razor-sharp sword was soon adopted by all seamen to inflict bloody wounds on their enemies.

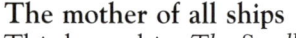

Corsairs' crowsfeet
French pirates had a cunning little weapon. They would throw these painfully sharp barbs onto the deck of the ship they were raiding so that the bare-footed sailors on the other side would tread on them.

Scary Vikings
The Vikings liked to parade their terrifying image of grisly and gruesome ferocity. They made carvings that would frighten their victims and boost their own confidence in battle.

Powder horn
Pirates stored small amounts of gunpowder in a powder horn, ready for battle. The main stock was stored in the ship's magazine, which was situated away from the hot stove in the galley – in case of explosive accidents.

Sharp surprise
Daggers were easy to carry as they were small and lightweight, and could be concealed under clothes for a surprise attack. In battle, pirates also wielded axes and cutlasses.

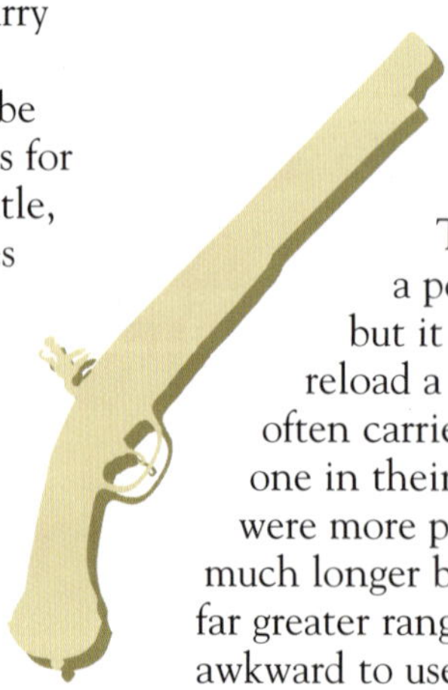

Fire power
The pistol was a popular weapon, but it took time to reload a gun, so pirates often carried more than one in their belts. Muskets were more powerful, had much longer barrels, and a far greater range, but were awkward to use in the thick of battle.

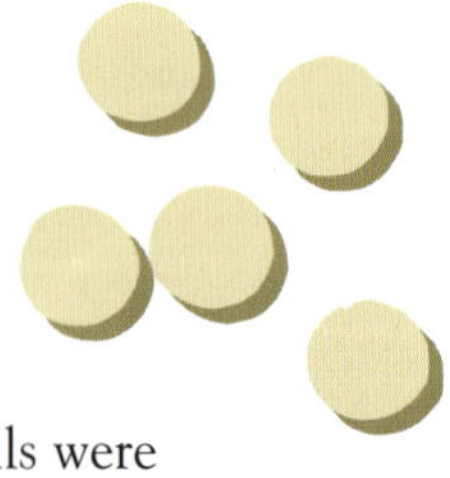

Small shot
Musket balls were wrapped in a cloth patch for a tight fit when loaded in the gun barrel. The musket fired one shot at a time, and was used to pick out individuals with a bit more accuracy than a blunderbuss.